CAPE
TOWN

CAPE TOWN

KATE NOAKES

 EYEWEAR PUBLISHING

First published in 2012
by Eyewear Publishing
74 Leith Mansions, Grantully Road
London W9 1LJ
United Kingdom

Typeset with graphic design by Edwin Smet
Author photograph Marie de Lutz
Printed in England by TJ International Ltd, Padstow, Cornwall

WWW.EYEWEARPUBLISHING.COM

4

To Paul, Charlotte and Angharad

'Perhaps it was history that ordained that it be here,
at the Cape of Good Hope that we should lay the
foundation stone of our new nation. For it was here at
this Cape, over three centuries ago, that there began the
fateful convergence of the peoples of Africa, Europe
and Asia on these shores.'

Nelson Mandela's inaugural speech, 1994

Kate Noakes
was born in Guildford of Welsh parentage.
She lived in Cape Town in 2011. This is her
third collection of poetry.

Table of Contents

Prologue
Hirundine — 8

I
Waking up in fairyland — 10
The barn swallow's carol — 11
The Snoek — 12
Number one shark watcher — 13
She-rain and the swallow — 14
Praise poem for the plastic chicken man — 15
Kenilworth racecourse to Dunsinane — 16
The Hedge — 17
Bonsai — 18
Flower sellers, De Waal Park — 19
Green Grass — 20
Central reservation equinox — 21
N2 desire paths — 22

II
Razor Wire — 24
The dictator's eyes — 25
Three Hurts — 27
Zonnebloem — 29
Ebrahim's Pigeons — 31
Split Estate — 33
The desert laughs — 34
Scarborough Anytown — 35
Transplant — 36
Radio Advertisement — 37
Lion's Head I — 38
Lion's Head II — 38
Kruger Nocturne — 39

Limpopo — 40
from the Cape Town bestiary
         — Baboon — 41
         — Guinea Fowl (helmeted) — 41
         — Hadedas — 42
         — White ibis and egrets — 42
         — A stone curlew for you — 43
A brownish background — 44
Harsh — 45
A Lift — 46

III

Kite surfing, Milnerton — 48
If I was — 49
This is Africa — 50
The scale of work — 51
On paying attention — 52
A change in the weather — 53
Green and yellow blanket man, Long Street — 54
On realising the South Pole is nearer to me than London
         by several thousand kilometres — 55
Burying the Hydra's tooth — 56
Reconciliation and the quagga — 57
Espresso, or the best cup of coffee in the world — 58
Signal Hill — 59
Paraphernalia, a found poem — 60
The dictator's last days — 61
Quagga — 63
Going to bed in fairyland — 64

Epilogue
Shabby land-song — 66

End notes — 68
Acknowledgements — 70

Hirundine

You'll know me by the broken wing
in my brain, the snapped swallow synapse,
the wrenched wrist bone on its torsion axis;

by the blue and the white of its coverts
and alulas as they stroke and scalpel
my head with secondaries and scattered down;

by the pent and twist of my energy flying
from one hemisphere to the other as I crook
my fingers and turn your milk to blood.

I

Waking up in fairyland

Call to prayer, and sprinklers pop up,
soak the garden before a blistering day.

The sun edges over the ring of hills,
over the known world. A red-winged starling

choruses on my balcony, beads of honey
in its throat. Sea fog blocks the city view.

A beach signpost explains muggings
in several languages. Guinea fowl squawk

and cackle on the back lawn.
The first cable car climbs the face

of the mountain. Bin people are out early
to recycle scraps: this morning

three rolls of unused wrapping paper
makes a toothless smile. News sellers

are at cross-roads and traffic lights.
The Big Issue has hit the streets.

The wheelchair-bound man with withered
legs readies a fresh coffee cup. The guy

who hawks metal sculptures of heron
and eagles is unloading his van.

A lump of crystal forms in my chest
as I glide by in a box full of radio.

The barn swallow's carol

Families gather, but as you come to sing
by the child's crib, I'm far off on the wing,
so long gone south-due-south into the Berg
wind, not hidden, torpid, not cold-air hung.

I don't know of hoar frost, or snow on snow
on snow. Earth-iron, water-stone
are mysteries. Bleak ice makes no moan.

I'm swallow, what gifts can I bring? Fat gnats,
thick mud, new nests from fynbos or Cape Flats.
Mid-winter/mid-summer, all I can I share:
the dip-dive, the soar-swoop in fresh-fly-air.

The Snoek

Boxed in my cell of glass
and steel, I catch the eye
of a passing woman.

She holds a yard of silver
by its tail, its head flops
where gills were cut,

blood dries from missing guts.
I point. Nice fish,
I mouthe.

She nods and smiles.
In another place
I might have got out for a chat.

In another place,
I'd have known
the name of the fish.

Number one shark watcher

He looks for the coming darkness, shadows
moving through the surf. A whole bay to scan,
but he knows the enemy, their territory:
he trawled the waters for twenty years,
a young man's game.

Now he fishes with a two-way radio
and polarising lenses. It's easier from the hill,
the angle cleaner, straight down
on those ever-moving shapes, never
dorsal fins breaking waves, never breaching
in the shallows. To swim free
of the world's only jumping sharks, don't
go out beyond that Norfolk pine, don't bleed,
don't mistake the white flag for peace.

She-rain and the swallow

There you are, fighting the south-easter
above my head, hovering,
buffeted high, then fast away.

It's been months. I've missed you.
The wires were empty,
just strings in the air, signalling nothing.

I need you to shiver and dance this
journey into whiteness, to help me laugh
and peep into this other world.

Let me keep small boys away,
their stones at bay. They know.
Their mothers have told them

not to pelt you with rocks.
You must be free to make rain
as I call out to you now, o friend,

and keep calling,
O friend, rain gently on me.
Bring me she-rain, a slow shower,

not bull-rain thundering onto its feet,
but the water that makes wild onions grow.

Praise poem for the plastic chicken man

All praise to you O plastic chicken man
with you dreads wound tight, locked in a round knot
of hair, today's scarf of silver threads lit
by the cross-roads sun.

                           Oh praise and praise again.

Oh praise to you my plastic chicken man
with your plump birds, full-breasted, fan-tailed
in red, yellow, blue.

                           But now you've
branched out into peacocks, flamingos,
acceded to fickle market demands:

Come fair-weather, come foul, comes the feather,
comes the fowl. I hope it works for you,
oh brightest of the bright plastic bird men.

Kenilworth racecourse to Dunsinane

The plant lady's at the gate again,
bends under white railings, takes the keen sward
of the track in her stride, stoops, and greens
her spade in the heath. She's stored pots
and compost, prepared, planned, primed.
Today is heather-rescue, a race.

Ericas cling nowhere save the middle
of the cinders, won't survive the whipping:
hooves, crowds, the detritus of the meet.
Re-homed, the ling is vulnerable-rare,
declining, endangered, extinct in the wild.
Its labels tell the story straight,
no spared punches, nothing mild.

The Hedge

I've watched a man coppice beech,
coax branches with his bill hook,
pin and fold living wood to his design,
trunk and twig, green leaves in time.

But here, hedge is boundary, thicket
for a half-moon of land and cattle are kept
safe to grow their meat and hides,
while the people stay on the outside;

a thorn and bramble fence
to hold darkness at arm's length,
filled with bitter, bitter almonds;
stockade that kills the common ground.

Yet, the truth is kept from me
as if I can't handle it. In half-stories
it's hidden, won't be spoken
till the right words can be chosen

for a plaque, placed full-square
into the bay, redrawn on the map.

Bonsai

This old man's hobby is my private pleasure
like yours is a collection of netsuke,
inro, ojime, less tactile in its raw, living form.

I can't weigh trees in my hand, though
if I could carry them in my pocket,
I surely would.

They won't find an easy home.
Will the children care? I can't think,
so must enjoy my hidden world,

stroll the garden with wine glass and scissors,
banish the day, a sip here, a snip there,
restore order; a small god with a watering can.

Flower sellers, De Waal Park

Precious knows where shade lasts all day,
how to keep proteas looking good in the heat,
how to stay comfortable on a plastic crate.

Today Grace has kilos of avos to sell,
each drawn up in a green string bag.
They line the curb like cups at prize giving.

It's too hot to speak. Precious out-stares
the ground, picks her palms, brushes leaves
and flies from her lap, makes a slow gesture.

Grace tries the closed window of the next car in the queue.

Green Grass
for Geoff

The pears are far, far too prickly here.
I've followed the ordinance for thirty years

barring durian fruit from tram and train,
lived on the minerals papaya contains.

Even though its seed-spice has peppered me,
kept me (knock on wood) care and cancer free,

like persimmons, nectarines, apricots,
they cannot loose my mouth, but just one bite

through taut skin into flesh that fizzes, spits,
foams fresh can do it – sweet-sour hiss hitting

my tongue with the scents of home; wild-flower
meadows in high summer, earthy winter

mud. Apples, when you ask what you can bring,
kilos please of Cox's Orange Pippins.

Central reservation equinox

Green in the southern suburbs, and nerines
trumpet change in leafless pinks.
Impossibly proud, they sway in the wind.

Under a knot of highways by the foreshore,
men sleep on cardboard and dirt.
They fight over blankets, bottles, tin foil.

Each morning, the man in a red acrylic jumper
is crouched by the metal barriers,
head in hands, shaking.

N2 desire paths

The highway is criss-crossed by paths you can't see,
tarmac resists shoe-prints. They join the dots
hard-shoulder to hard-shoulder, dry lines
marking verges behind graffitied shacks,
picked out over litter and the hoof prints of goats.

These rights of passage are the quickest way
from hole in the fence A to ditto B,
crow-flights on the ground, no matter the cars
in early dark, the rush-crush of the hour,
crash barriers, signs, white lines, no matter
public radio advice, neon lights,
the law, the what-is-it-for...

They're fast lanes to school or shop
or shebeen, even if shoes can't wear
through stone and tar, the paths are there,
want attention, don't stop
at the central reservation, need you
to stay awake, to see them in time.

II

Razor Wire

I walk the razed section of the city
looking at brown grass, bricks, concrete.

Plastic bags tatter against the chain link.
The late afternoon sun cuts the air slant.

A man thrusts his hand through a gap,
braves its metal thorns to shake mine.

It's soft, unexpected from the grazes
on his arms, his face, the missing

chunk of his nose.
Here, here, my sister, welcome.

The dictator's eyes

When he was young,
the dictator saw everything
with perfect clarity,
twenty: twenty.
He had vision.

Some years passed,
a decade or two,
and the dictator began
to complain: he couldn't see
around corners,

no longer had eyes
in the back of his head.
On rare days
when he drove himself,
he had trouble parking the car.

He said it was as if
he was in a tunnel, light
and the world further away.
A decade or two passed.
The dictator woke up

one morning unable to see
wife number five's face
or the blue irises at his bedside.
Cataracts, the doctor
told his only patient.

The dictator was driven
to the airport in dark glasses
behind the tinted windows
of a white limousine.
Without a care

he heaved onto the counter
a suitcase full of money
(used notes, foreign)
and asked for
a friendly destination.

Three Hurts

One has wrapped itself,
over and over,
like barbed wire.

It has two spikes
to rip you again
if you get too close.

Two is the shredder
of flesh on garden fences
from Jo'burg to the Cape:

razor wire,
the precursor
of an armed response.

Three is electric, thin,
mean, keeps you
in your place

like cattle or sheep.
It's always there, droning,
hard to switch off.

But, like Daphne,
you can cover these
wounds with new bark,

draw them
into your heartwood.
In time they will rust

and flake, season
your growth, even
gloss your crown.

Zonnebloem

Hold fast to dreams for if dreams die, life is a broken-winged bird that cannot fly —
LANGSTON HUGHES

Let me tell you how I fill my nostrils with home,
with the girls at the hairdresser, their teenage primping
and perms, pink curlers, hot tongs,

                        or the boys
at the barbers stopping by for a smoke and a shave
or short-back-and-sides,

                        and of the choirs,
crooners, jazz bands, their music before it browned,
of football teams and days in the park,

the bandstand and churches, gang fights
down this alley or that, preserved now
in black and white,

                        and let me tell you
of all the places we went between home and school,
home and mosque, home and synagogue,

I can point to them on the map,

                        and of baking
and braais or fires on patches of wasteland,
and of the junk and rubbish,

dust and old tyres, the whole wonderful
mess of it, of our teachers, crane-operators,
maids, nurses,

                        stevedores — fairyland.

You can see the street names here so we don't
forget them: shepherd, lesar, clifton,

godfrey, parkins, arundel, hamilton,
windsor, tennant, cambridge, constitution,
join me in thanking the man

                                    who saved them
from the bay, and let the other signs
remind you I'm not inventing.

'I am every stone in this place of stones'.

Now throw open the doors, un-cramp this city
from pews and stained glass, let these voices
shout down the street

                                    over yellow grass,
lumps of concrete. I can see bricks stacking up,
wooden stakes forcing their way

into baked earth. There's the smell of creosote,
emulsion on the breeze.
Sunflowers are cracking tarmac.

Ebrahim's Pigeons

We take them to Noordhoek in the back
of Mohammed, the butcher's, bakkie,
the scenic way past Bay and Peak
to the long stretch of curving white,

accommodating the sea. We release them
in the car park, watch them circle, glide,
compass through moments of wild,
mapping mountain, plotting peninsula.

While they are all air speed and position,
we stroll the sand to the wreck, drive home
in time to see them make it to the yard-loft,
their breasts heaving with effort.

*

Last of all my beauties are packed
into five old wicker baskets, ten abreast
for the ride to the new place. I won't
call it home. The truck rumbles

over patched streets. I fret as they jostle
each other. I'd mourn if they broke.
It takes a month for me to finish
their new crees. Pleasing, the day I tuck

them in. Their song that night is rounded,
content and I sleep in deep-bellied comfort.
We drive south on a windless day,
as before, set them free to wheel, flock

and gather for the return leg. I watch them
head over fynbos and rock,
taking my time at the shore, they know
where they're going.

I pace the patch of scrubby grass
my wife calls lawn (yes, we have a garden
in Athlone), but not one, not yet.
A couple of spotted neighbourhood

birds rough over. They aren't my lovelies,
my doves. The sun goes. Not one. I ready
for prayer, for bed. Not one, yet.
In morning's dark it hits me.

Not here. I find them pecking
brick dust, splinters of wood, all that is left
in Caledon Street. Athlone isn't home
to them, to us, not one, not yet.

Split   Estate

Fracking	will mean years of asking what's true	F
racking	will give us energy anew	Fr
acking	will break the land with its ju-ju	Fra
cking	will do more than spoil more than a great view	Frac
king	will poison rivers with CO_2	Frack
ing	will fill sinks and showers with glue	Fracki
ng	will leave you lost, now what to do?	Frackin
g	will kill you, you and the Karoo.	Fracking

The desert laughs

with each of its footfalls, each crescent
of sand that banks across the fertile hills,
storming wells, waterholes and gardens with glass.

We sing the old songs on our march south,
songs of plump dates and plenty,
of fig and pomegranate, yet we can't shake off

our veils or bell-hung hats. We no longer know
whose plan it was to fell that stand,
up-root the last acacias,

but we suspect horned and vengeful gods
with tooth-edged flails. No-one remembers
the names of the birds in the tree of eyes,

all I can see is sap gushing like blood,
futile sacrifice; the bark-gods powerless,
resigned, so small; and our speechless mothers

embracing the axe, dancing with bundles
of sticks round their necks, their bracelets
knelling an ivory beat; the grass singing dirges

under their feet. O this present heat,
this dust, this haze of namib we've made
for sidewinder and sun. No shade, no aloes

here for the healing, just ancient plants,
welwitschia, and one dove, namaqua,
an impossible leaf in its bill.

Scarborough Anytown

A lone ostrich runs his fence line,
keeps up as we leave the village.

You point to an abandoned plot
fynbos revivifies with ericas,
geraniums, thatching grass.

Before was the house a Swiss family
built in stages, lonely work
battening a roof yourself,

fretting weather boards, firing
window-boxes with pelargoniums
all the shades of scarlet.

A hot summer, the veldt, tinder;
the burn over the hill lit three houses
(never buy a home at the margins).

Transplant

Too late for us, but somewhere in a building
of corridors, tolleys, bleach, you pause –
certain 'it's going to work', or a little scared
your oath might fail, this brave man won't live
to tell. You steady your hands,

scrub them till perfectly clean: backs,
fronts, nails, forearms almost raw,
not one fold of skin spared the brush.
They are steady for the first incision
through quiet flesh,

firm for the force of rib-crack and chest-
spread, steady again for the cut, hold, tie
of arteries, veins; most steady
for the fist-sized miracle of muscle
you graft with gut-string and blood-glue.

Could you have been a decade quicker?
If you'd saved Grandpa with your busy knife
and careful fingers, we'd have applauded too.

Radio Advertisement

Not mother but child,
yes, we can make a free generation.

We can change the red and the white,
take out the poison, mother to child,
erase all sign of it from neighbourhood rocks

and the hard face of the roadside,
clean shop windows, re-paste bill boards
for mother and child. See how we sharpen

our pencils, fill pens with fresh ink,
wash brushes, bathe mother and child.
We can fix the symbol, round it to infinity,

make it whole like child with mother,
close shelters for all the right reasons.
It starts with you, you mother, your child.

Yes, we can make a generation
of infinities, an infinity for life.

Lion's Head I

Much depends on the red
helicopter beating its wings:
the day too hot for a stony path,
that second bottle of wine at the top,
the fast descent over loose rock,
too hot for your heart –
tick-tock, tick-tock.

Lion's Head II

Full moon, a chain of fireflies
winds down the mountain,
step by drunken step.

I watch for flashes of light,
strain for cries, think
of the helicopter blind on its H.

Kruger Nocturne

In the falling-dark it seems impossible
to spot game disappeared in the bush,
but our torches find the backs of eyes
and we scan until retinas give away
hippo foraging in the watery dark, miles
from river and hyacinth cover;
a dark-striped civet intent on a mouse;
a nightjar snug to ground churring, purring,
churring to the feathered dark;
Duke, the bent-tusked elephant,
the thick dark concealing his bulk;
and a pair of lionesses out hunting
who pause to test the shiver of us
in the cooling dark of the jeep and trot away
tamping the dust and starry dark.
Sharing boerewors from our braai, we turn
to darker matters: the Southern Cross,
the Milky Way, the whole night sky.

Limpopo

Guards look away for cool-drink-money, one more soul
slips the bounds of Zim, slides over the greasy-green
into a land of maybes (I won't say promises) –
Luck has found the outer-side of the Kruger fence
unlike the last group flesh-picked by hyenas,
papers, clothes, bones scattered in the unknown bush.

He walks with hope, walks collecting dust and blisters.
A week, and so he comes to an informal stretch
where pallets, tarps and sheets of corrugated tin
can be called a house, if gang-sprayed might have colour.
Not 'shackland to dignity'. No shack. No shack. No.

He rests on hard earth behind those kilometres
of huts, hungry, alone, eyes wide on the heavens;
one star strung out along the freeway, just-dreaming of a roof.

from the Cape Town bestiary

Baboon

Baboons are dangerous wild animals. Do not feed. Keep doors locked and windows closed.
Street signage, Muizenburg

Fred is quite himself: curious, quick-witted,
light-fingered, a gang leader, hungry, smart,
cheeky, a gourmand, trained in culinary art.

Fred is shot by locals grown tired of his
walk-on, run-on part, thinking of tourists
and their ever-thinning hearts.

Fred, the baboon, is shot. Visitors need other
distractions: patisserie, good bread, pesto,
goat's cheese and walnut tarts.

Guinea Fowl (helmeted)

make a point of coming down the mountain
to bookend my day with their raucous calls
as if I'm a slouch or dirty stop out.

If they're not careful, they'll have their spots
knocked off. I've heard they're interesting
and, like much else, taste of chicken.

Hadedas

The cricket pitch is freshly seeded. Sprinklers
run at full tilt. We are told to keep off.

Hadedas can't read. Thirty birds
spike the grass for worms, oblivious
on the first cool evening of March.

It gives me time to catch them,
not all dun or grey; in the creases
of their wings green iridescence rises.

White ibis and egrets

Pre-open air Shakespeare
and a crowd is busy
with picnics and wine.

I'm the only one
watching a host of white,
ibis and cattle egrets

lengthen the branches
of a lakeside willow,
quiet ghouls at rest,

green wood crying
under the burden,
impossible for more

to find room, yet
they jostle in,
ghosting the tree

into a sacrament
of handkerchiefs
and saintly prayers.

A stone curlew for you

On the hem of the hill tonight, a Cape Dippock,
stilted on the verge, statue with wide eyes,
shocked from shore or scrub,
steadies my gaze,
readies itself for the avoidances of dark.
There goes the last note of evensong.

Later, two men bird-watch indoors.
The world premiere of Fugard's new play
opens with an epiphany:
mamma and baby birds, look, Cape Dippocks.

A brownish background

Quagga theory says this is what develops
when you stop making negative distinctions

between, say, Grey's zebra with its plain belly,
black body, thin stripes,
                              and the smaller Burchell's
with wide stripes and shadow stripes extending
around its belly,
                              or look to the endangered
Mountain zebra, white belly, stripes widening over its rump.

Quagga theory says they are all gregarious,
all neck wrestle and bite to protect what's theirs.

Each animal uniquely patterned,
bar-coded for its foals to find home.

Harsh

The birds are plagued by smoker's coughs,
rough-tongued, hammer-tongued, voices shred
the air as if barbed wire. Mellifluous is not
a word for sand-throated, sharp-throated
song, squawks, cackles, the dashing of tar
on stone. This is a drill.

Pigeons, of course, are pigeons, the same
the world over, but there's an edge
to their coos. They too know pot-holes.
The chorus is road-digging, road-mending.
A roller of alarm; an emergency wanting
attention is just around the corner.

A Lift

Waiting road-side would be a bad idea.
I no longer have the energy to ask why
(to avoid a drive-by?).

We trek back into the bush
to a likely stand of shrub. It's hot.
Mica sand, scoured from the rock

and wind-piled is cool, cold even,
like the company. Sleep is the only thing
to do this hour. Empty bottles

and scrunched foil make my rucksack
a poor pillow. My dream is rich
with bird-song and car hum

and the hiss of a Cape cobra attending
to his acre of scrub, rear-guarding
so we know he's there.

III

Kite surfing, Milnerton

Bright against blue, kites in lime green
and deep vermillion spin their riders

to the dredger, a collage of rust-orange,
rust-brown, its three yellow cranes;

obstacle between dangerous beach
and the island. The surfers might be slammed

by a furious wind. Or, if not hazard,
then race point: round-the-ship-and-back

whatever-the-wind-or-tide, I might have
heard, but the wind is the kind that silences

the day, takes your voice, un-hears
your companions, rescuers, hides

the sun's heat in its mouth and spits
at you from turquoise water. Hanging on

is all that is needed, that and the ability to angle,
judge fury, hold its sway, twist, turn,

board aloft or crushing white horses. I can see
energy being spent right here, but the wind

makes it effortless and the kites nothing more
than a flight of birds, pelicans perhaps.

If I was

to be wave-caught again, tossed
from my board, roughed into the sea,
I would take a deeper breath
and hold it longer,

        and if I could know
I would make it, I might not see
my short life in a flash of sand pits
and sandwich boxes, see-saws and swings,

I might dissolve into the water,
slipping from sky to sea, white
overhead, the uncertain angle
of the sea bed.

        And if I could trust
myself and the sea, I might brush off
the scratch and scrape of sand
as I am dumped at the water's edge,

drawn back, let free, breathless
on the beach, both hands clawing shingle.
If I could, I might enjoy it.

This is Africa

Aloes in the low veldt, miles of dry, red earth
over-grazed, empty land, Overberg,

low density sheep, cattle, a few ostriches
in dusty yards, white farm houses,

tin roofs, a pied crow, a pair of blue cranes,
wind in the eucalypts sounding rain,

a spent condom in the scatter of picnic debris,
a distant controlled burn, random flies,

proteas releasing their seeds,

no-one about save three smartly-dressed blokes
at the side of the road, one pushes a bike,

has some way, somewhere to go
unlike the woman squatting next to her heavy load.

The scale of work

Emperor penguins are tall
about four foot. My friend is small
in the world – less than five,
confirmed on a single purpose trip to the zoo,

which is like saying this toad
is the size of my head,
though it's burrowed deep for brain food,
squatted long enough to slick my hair with wax and toxin.

It's time it was piped out to the coast road
to take its chances.

On paying attention

They emerge when autumn's rains begin
and fill the pavements with song.
For all I know they're like Selborne swallows
rising from ponds in a British spring,
or American cicadas every seventeen years
transmogrifying soil.

For now they're tree-frogs
hiding in greenery at the picture-house,
stretching their throats in the night air
to drum a chorus of Look at me,
No, me, No, me...

but I'm mistaken, May's crickets
are all legs, taut as gut-strings,
a concerto of blow-ins for my night
promenades that coils into cello sleep
like the tight necks of double basses.

A change in the weather

Cloud comes in to clear the air of dust and plant oil,
eucalyptus, pine, leaves it sweet, autumnal,
rolls down the mountain, floats in from the sea,
fills the Nek and gorges with spots of wet.

In come The Others, in comes eerie.

Fog horns sound all night in the bay, blasting out
their one note song. The lighthouse lamp picks up
speed, mist-fuelled, and all the floating buoys
wink as if glitter balls in a mad disco.

Green and yellow blanket man, Long Street

There's no-one who can
ruin my day quite like the green
and yellow blanket man

because I am rich with coins,
because I am ugly,
because I have big feet for a woman,
because I am a bitch

to which I say
fuck off-you-aggressive-little-beggar-bugger,
but only in my head.

On realising the South Pole is nearer to me than London
by several thousand kilometres

Twenty-odd-miles to the absolute Cape
to the two masses of water clashing
in perpetual confusion: currents, tide,
where hope may as well be abandoned
to lighthouse and storm; I'm about as far
as it's possible for the road to go.
It feels good to be at The End –

There's one direction now, back
the way I've come, the road north,
the road more travelled.
Anything else would plunge me
into ice floes, the shrinking land of blue
and numbness. I might be nearer
to it than home, but attractions pale.

I must turn the other-way-up, and soon.

Burying the Hydra's tooth

Monday, under my office desk
I found a tooth, not a first one
lost by a child on Saturday seeing
where Daddy works, milky, innocent,
but an adult molar, bloody-rooted, part-decayed.
I tossed it into the bin.

A rasp of leaves, a rustle and huff made me break off
mid-sentence that afternoon and peer in.

A young puff adder was coiled like a ribbed spring.
It stared at me with diamond eyes
and certain, terrible knowledge.

Reconciliation and the quagga

The quagga-trick is knowing your place
in the active sweat of forgetting and selecting,

what to keep and what to loose,
what to cover and how to choose;

when to let a shot gun bruise with rust,
and when to oil its metal with ooze.

When to schmooze the next dictator
with dead set views on shooting his mouth

with old songs that once had their use,
but are no longer new,

how to show him and his crew
the yellow diamonds on their shoes

and when to say, the quagga is through.

Espresso, or the best cup of coffee in the world

will be served in a small white china cup
with thick sides to hold its heat
on a small white china saucer
with vestigial white paper coaster,
you may be about to drink it even now;

will be so concentrated it sticks
like treacle or molasses
and will be the same colour as both,
as if water is rationed, beans two-a-penny;
will test you: lemon rind wiped round the rim,
one lump, two or nothing at all?

and when you lift it to your lips
and sip, any minute now,
will rush through you
like happiness, like all those things
for which there are no words.

Signal Hill

The contour map of the hill,
a finger print, a whorl of furrowed skin,
tells me there is only one of me,
cuts and lines are how you tell me apart.

And so I wait until the day (make it soon)
when on the dot of the Noon Gun
you'll come with tickets
and inky palms to fetch me home.

Paraphernalia, a found poem

Tell me this is normal: eating strawberries
in the necropolis where Angolans are playing football,
morning in the burned house, evening brings everything back,
the unreliable mushrooms, the watermelon man,
telling each other it is possible.

Aubergine is a gravid woman, a two-part invention
home and away, the miracle diet, what she did
and what she said, her name like the hours self-made.
And in here the menagerie: birds through a ceiling
of alabaster, ghosts at cockcrow, horses where answers
would have been like something flying backwards.

Can you hear, bird, the weather coming?
The banking thing, the back and forth of it,
the way the money goes, you again learning how to fall,
how to disappear, take me with you.

The dictator's last days

He asked for a friendly destination
where they (couldn't see death
in the back of his eyes) might find
him exotic, worldly-wise.

There was only one atoll left,
a stretch of hot, white sand
hemmed by wind-straggled palms;
a luxurious place to be alone.

For a few years he enjoyed exercise,
climbing the hill to see his little
piece of turquoise and azure sea,
watch dolphins bouncing beyond

the reef, count waves sequencing
surf. He made a massive collection
of shells, mostly conch. They reminded
him of those who used to speak;

he found new ways to pile
and pole them. When his orange suit
fell apart, he fashioned a grass skirt,
strung a necklace with fronds

and chicken bones, thought about
piercing his nose. After a few more years
his Shakespeare was thin, its pages
rubbed through by his thumb,

his bible pristine, if sandy. One week
the captain asked if there was anything,
anything at all. A gun and single bullet
were supplied, a last kindness, a pleasure.

Quagga

Quagga-me says wind me anti-clockwise.

Before the run of cars, stand me in first light
with last night's chip-bags and Carling cans
outside Vivienne Westwood's shop

(1983, World's End, Chelsea) in front of thirteen hours
and backwards-running hands.
Dress me in half-stripes: black, white, brown.

A forlorn mare, head dropped, cowed,
is the only photograph of a real quagga
(Regent's Park Zoo, 1870).

No pictures of me as the dandy pirate;
I made sure to avoid instamatics, I've been able to chose
whether or not to have been there, anywhere.

The last quagga died in Amsterdam
in 1883, although it wasn't me until recently.
I'm just not that kind of horse.

The empty land is too dry, too dusty,
nor do I fancy Louis XVI's menagerie.
The new quagga is not me either.

You can't breed-back anymore than you can unpick
twenty three stuffed quaggas, un-tan hides,
un-digest meat. You can't avoid tsetse flies.

You can't, in the end, turn back the clock.

Going to bed in fairyland

Sun leaves the City Bowl an hour before
sea sink; that's Signal Hill for you.

A late runner comes off the mountain
sweating. Yogis practise peace.

All the lights come on in the gloaming,
pattern highways and low-ways

with silver and gold. The cable car stops.
Commuters queue to go over the Nek.

Before the quiet of pine roosts, guinea fowl
quarrel. Blouberg lighthouse blinks miles

into my sitting room. Peacocks strut
the stairwell. Braziers at Cafe Paradiso are lit.

Car guards change shift or their neon vests.
Minibuses jostle for Mitchell's plain.

Ticket sellers take to their booths at
the Labia, Baxter, Fugard; Athol showcases

his new play. Pop corn pops. Slush-puppies
churn bright blue, the colour of raspberries.

Hibscus blooms close as tight as trumpets.
Cacti flowers open for organ-playing moths.

The cube-tray of crystal in my chest melts
as I slide the jet-way towards the scent

of home: a waft of brewer's yeast,
brick grime, my garden in spring.

Epilogue

Shabby land-song

So sigh here, or shine then my straight-stretch of sea,
all slate and silver shod, my shrapnel rocks stacked
slant, my shy grass shivering before the scythe,

my schist and sliver of sky, its shawl of cloud,
my shut sorrel path and strew-stone slopes,
my roadside shrine of squid graffiti, shade signs
of stag and toad, my sheep shank swimming,

shingle squeaks and shale-sand shouts, the shift
and shunt of skin shoulders me in among a thousand
shuddering voices, show-singing or swan shrieking
from small sheets of hearth, heath, health.

End notes

Waking up (and going to bed) in fairyland and **Zonnebloem** - Fairyland was the name given to District Six (now Zonnebloem), Cape Town in graffiti on a no longer extant house wall. The inhabitants of District Six (a mixed race, working class district of the central city) were forcibly evicted under the Group Areas Act. Their houses were demolished. Much of the area remains a wasteland, although there is a partial rebuilding programme underway and some former residents and their families have returned. Zonnebloem is Afrikaans for sunflower.

She-rain and the swallow - In the folk lore of the San people, the original inhabitants of the Western Cape, swallows make she-rain.

The Hedge - Jan van Riebeeck, commander of the Dutch East India company, had planted a wild almond hedge many kilometres in length in 1660 to protect the Cape colony. It is considered the first act of Apartheid. Its remnants can be seen at Kirstenbosch and Bishop's Court.

Transplant - Dr Christiaan Barnard performed the world's first heart transplant at Groote Schuur hosptial, Cape Town in December 1967.

Radio Advertisement was inspired by SAFM public service advertising for the prevention of mother to child HIV/AIDS transmission.

Lion's Head is a precipitous peak next to Table Mountain.

Kruger Nocturne is set in the Kruger National Park in the north east of South Africa.

Ebrahim's Pigeons is based on a true story told by one of the forcibly moved residents of District Six.

Kite surfing, Milnerton - Robben Island can be seen from Milnerton beach.

Quagga - Equus quagga quagga, an extinct sub-species of plains zebra from the Karoo. Since 1986 there has been a selective rebreeding programme in South Africa with a view to possible reintroduction into the wild.

Acknowledgements

I am grateful to Philip Gross for his invaluable advice on the manuscript, Jason McGimsey for his eagle eyes and the people of Cape Town for giving me their stories.

Earlier versions of some of these poems have appeared in *The SHOp* ('Green and yellow blanket man', 'Long Street', 'Praise poem for the plastic chicken man'); *Ink Sweat + Tears* ('Zonnebloem'); *Gumbo Press* ('Espresso, or the best cup of coffee in the world'); *The Interpreter's House* ('On paying attention'); and *Iota* ('The desert laughs', 'Green Grass'). I thank the editors of these publications here.